LET'S TALK SPORTS!

TALK LIKE A
HOCKEY PLAYER

BY RYAN NAGELHOUT

Gareth Stevens
PUBLISHING

Please visit our website, www.garethstevens.com. For a free color catalog of all our high-quality books, call toll free 1-800-542-2595 or fax 1-877-542-2596.

Cataloging-in-Publication Data

Names: Nagelhout, Ryan.
Title: Talk like a hockey player / Ryan Nagelhout.
Description: New York : Gareth Stevens Publishing, 2017. | Series: Let's talk sports! | Includes index.
Identifiers: ISBN 9781482457049 (pbk.) | ISBN 9781482457063 (library bound) | ISBN 9781482457056 (6 pack)
Subjects: LCSH: Hockey–Juvenile literature. | Hockey players–Juvenile literature.
Classification: LCC GV847.25 N34 2017 | DDC 796.962–dc23

First Edition

Published in 2017 by
Gareth Stevens Publishing
111 East 14th Street, Suite 349
New York, NY 10003

Designer: Samantha DeMartin
Editor: Ryan Nagelhout

Photo credits: Title art chudo-yudo/Shutterstock.com; series background Supphachai Salaeman/Shutterstock.com; cover, p. 1 inset Adam Vilimek/Shutterstock.com; cover, p. 1 hockey player Valeriy Lebedev/Shutterstock.com; puck caption stockphoto-graf/Shutterstock.com; p. 4 Vaclav Volrab/Shutterstock.com; p. 5 Val Thoermer/Shutterstock.com; p. 6 SebStock/Shutterstock.com; p. 7 Nagel Photography/Shutterstock.com; pp. 8, 21 CarpathianPrince/Shutterstock.com; p. 9 Sean Rudyk/National Hockey League/Getty Images; p. 10 Minnitre/Shutterstock.com; p. 11 Bruce Bennett/Getty Images Sport/Getty Images; p. 13 Hero Images/Getty Images; p. 14 indigolotos/Shutterstock.com; p. 15 Andy Devlin/National Hockey League/Getty Images; p. 16 (bottom) Steve Russell/Toronto Star/Getty Images; p. 16 (top) Shell114/Shutterstock.com; p. 17 Isantilli/Shutterstock.com; p. 19 Gregg Forwerck/National Hockey League/Getty Images; p. 23 Aspen Photo/Shutterstock.com; p. 25 Ronald Martinez/Getty Images Sport/Getty Images; p. 26 Shooter Bob Square Lenses/Shutterstock.com; p. 27 Jonathan Kozub/National Hockey League/Getty Images; p. 28 pavle75/Shutterstock.com; p. 29 The Washington Post/The Washington Post/Getty Images.

Printed in the United States of America

CPSIA compliance information: Batch #CW17GS : For further information contact Gareth Stevens, New York, New York at 1-800-542-2595.

CONTENTS

Words in the glossary appear in **bold** type the first time they are used in the text.

ICE UP!

What do you know about hockey? Maybe you've played it on a street with friends. You probably know the **professionals** play it on ice. But if you want to take to the ice yourself, you need to know how to talk hockey.

THERE ARE LOTS OF DIFFERENT TERMS PEOPLE USE IN HOCKEY. IT'S A GAME THAT HAS ITS OWN LANGUAGE!

Hockey played outside on flat surfaces is called street hockey. It's called roller hockey if people wear special shoes with wheels called inline skates.

Do you know what icing is? Or do you know what it means when a player scores a "hat trick"? Let's take a look at some of the language hockey players use so you can talk like a hockey player!

TO THE RINK

Hockey is a game played on a sheet of ice at a hockey rink. The rink is 200 feet (61 m) long and 85 feet (26 m) wide. The rink is curved at the ends to create an oval shape. Walls called boards circle the rink to keep the players inside.

BOARDS

LEARN THE LINGO

A yellow band of **fiberglass** runs along the bottom of the boards. This is called a kickplate. The rest of the boards are white, with a red ring at the top before the glass.

HIT THE GLASS

Early hockey rinks had wire fencing above the boards. Today, rinks are circled by special kinds of glass that let fans see what's happening on the ice. The ends of the rink are lined with a kind called Plexiglas, and the sides use **tempered** glass.

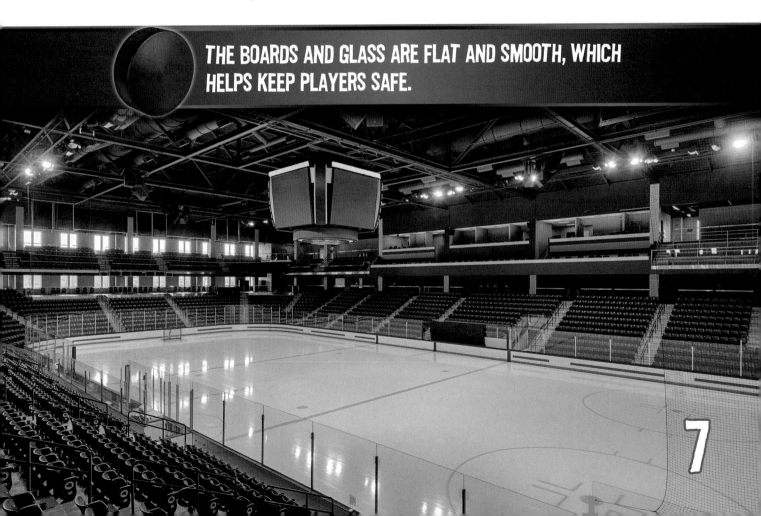

THE BOARDS AND GLASS ARE FLAT AND SMOOTH, WHICH HELPS KEEP PLAYERS SAFE.

PAINT ON THE ICE

A red line runs down the middle of each ice rink. This is center ice. Two blue lines mark each team's offensive zone, or where they try to score goals. There are also red face-off dots in different spots on the ice.

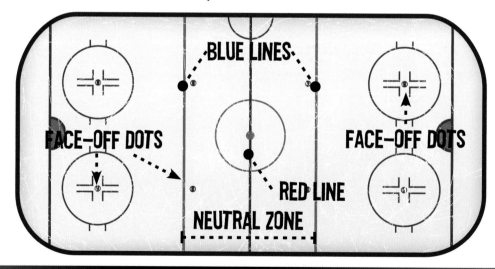

BLUE LINES

FACE-OFF DOTS

FACE-OFF DOTS

RED LINE

NEUTRAL ZONE

THIS IS WHAT A STANDARD HOCKEY RINK LOOKS LIKE. MOST THINGS ARE PAINTED RED OR BLUE, THOUGH LOGOS AND OTHER MARKINGS CAN BE PAINTED BY EACH TEAM.

DROP THE PUCK

Face-offs start every play in hockey. A **referee** drops the puck in the middle of the rink—center ice—after a goal or to start a period. If play is stopped, the next face-off happens at the closest face-off circle.

LEARN THE LINGO

One team's offensive zone is the other's defensive zone. The middle of the ice between the blue lines is called the **neutral** zone.

9

PUCKS

The most important thing in hockey is the puck. It's a disk of **vulcanized** rubber players chase during a game. The first use of the word "puck" was in the *Montreal Gazette* on February 7, 1876. Early pucks were made of frozen cow dung and sliced-up lacrosse balls!

ABOUT A DOZEN PUCKS ARE USED DURING THE AVERAGE PRO HOCKEY GAME.

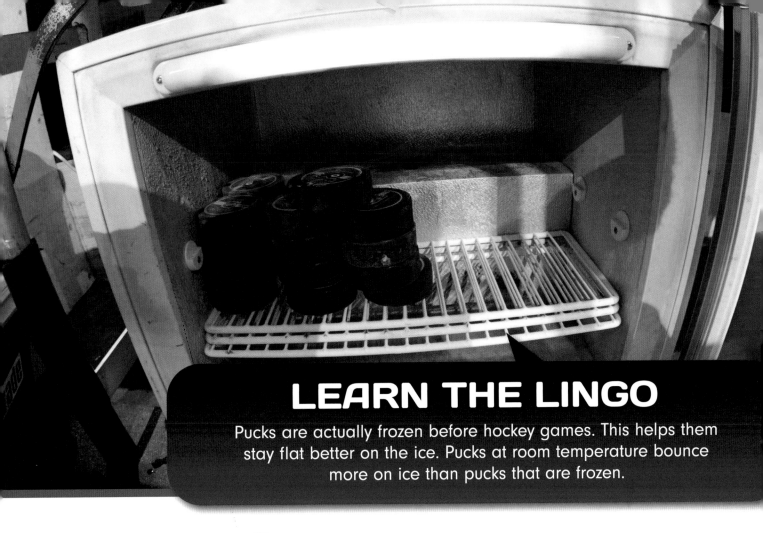

LEARN THE LINGO

Pucks are actually frozen before hockey games. This helps them stay flat better on the ice. Pucks at room temperature bounce more on ice than pucks that are frozen.

WHAT'S IT CALLED?

There are many other names for the puck in hockey.

Some people call it a "biscuit" because it looks a bit like a burnt dinner roll.

11

HIT THE NET

To score a goal, you have to get the puck past your **opponent**'s goalie. A goalie in hockey is sometimes called a goaltender or netminder. This is because they try to stop shots aimed at the net by the other team. They actually "tend to" or "mind" the net!

IN THE BLUE

The area in front of the net is called the crease. It's painted blue, and it's the goalie's area. Players on the other team can't bump into the goalie in the crease!

LEARN THE LINGO

The crease starts at the red line, or goal line, in front of the net. The puck must cross this line to be ruled a goal.

CREASE

GOAL LINE

THE CREASE CAN BE DIFFERENT SIZES AND EVEN DIFFERENT SHAPES AT SOME LEVELS OF HOCKEY.

STICKS AND SKATES

SHAFT

Hockey **equipment** is different from the equipment in most sports. Each player uses a stick to move the puck. The stick has a long thin rod, called a shaft, that the player holds. The end of the stick is bent and flat. This is called the blade.

LEARN THE LINGO

Hockey sticks are sometimes called "twigs" because they were first made of wood.

BLADE

CAREY PRICE DEFENDS THE NET WITH HIS STICK.

BIGGER STICKS

Goalie sticks are wider and shorter than other sticks.

That's because they're not used to shoot, but to block more of the net to keep players from scoring.

15

Hockey players don't wear shoes—they wear skates. Skates are boots with sharp blades on the bottom that **glide** on ice. This helps players skate very fast. They can turn their feet and dig these blades into the ice to stop quickly.

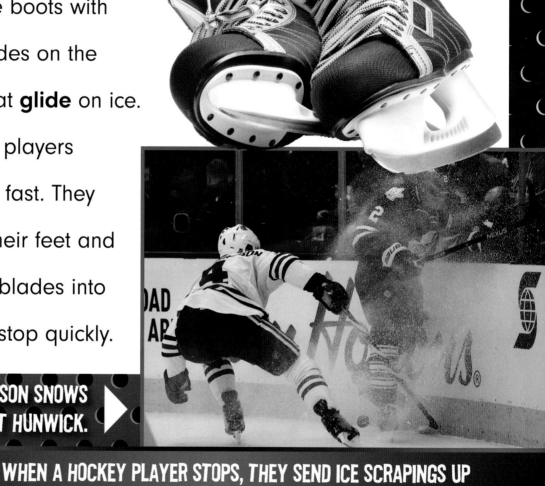

NIKLAS HJALMARSSON SNOWS MATT HUNWICK. ▶

WHEN A HOCKEY PLAYER STOPS, THEY SEND ICE SCRAPINGS UP INTO THE AIR. SOMETIMES THEY "SNOW" SOMEONE, OR SPRAY THEM WITH ICE PIECES, ON PURPOSE!

LEARN THE LINGO

Goaltenders wear different skates than other players. They also wear much more padding to stay safe from blades, sticks, and hard shots!

STAYING SAFE

Skate blades are sharpened so they better cut into the ice. To keep from being cut, players wear special gloves and other equipment, called pads.

17

SHOOT AND SCORE

Scoring goals and stopping goals are the two most important things in hockey. But how do you put the biscuit (puck) in the basket (net)? There are a few different ways to shoot the puck on goal. The first is called a wrist shot. This is a quick shot where the player uses their wrists to snap the puck into the goal.

LEARN THE LINGO

Slap shots and wrist shots are taken on the forehand, or using the front of the stick. A backhand shot is taken using the other side.

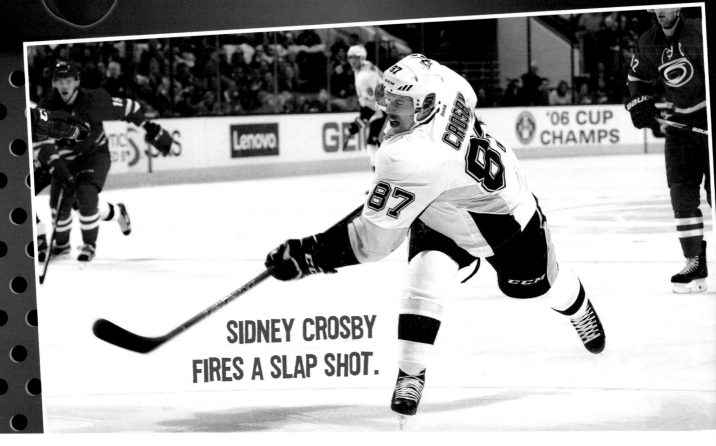

SIDNEY CROSBY FIRES A SLAP SHOT.

SLAP IT

Another is a slap shot. This is a hard shot where a player swings their stick back and then brings it down, slapping the puck forward.

19

KNOW THE POSITION

In hockey, each team has six players on the ice. Five players are skaters, and one is the goaltender. Out of the five skaters, two are defenders and three are forwards. Defenders, also called defensemen, work together in pairs. One plays the left side of the ice, while the other plays the right.

LEARN THE LINGO

Wingers usually play with the same teammates at the same time. The wingers and center are called a "line" and come onto the ice as a group.

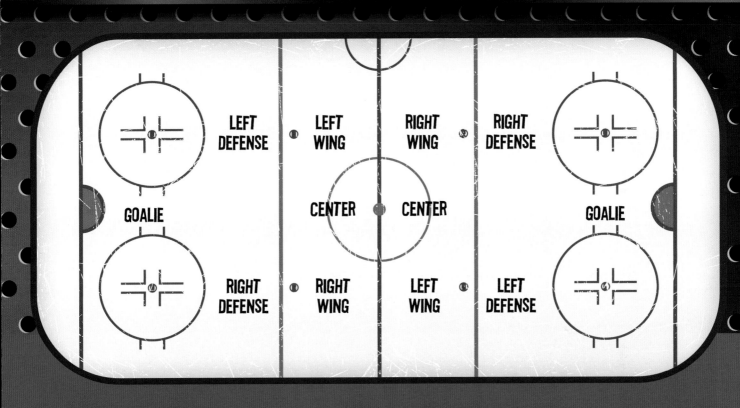

LEFT, RIGHT, AND CENTER

Forwards are either left wingers, right wingers, or centers. Left and right wingers play on each side of the ice. Centers play in the middle of the ice and take face-offs.

21

PERIODS

Hockey games are split up into three parts called periods. In professional hockey, each period lasts 20 minutes. Between each period is a break, called intermission. In the National Hockey League, this break is 18 minutes long.

CLEAN IT UP

During each intermission, people clean off the ice for the next period. A large machine called a resurfacer scrapes the top of the ice and puts water down, which freezes again to make new ice!

LEARN THE LINGO

Most people call the ice resurfacer a Zamboni. That's because Frank Zamboni invented the ice resurfacer and started a company that sells the machines. Other companies make "zambonis," though.

ZAMBONI

HOCKEY IS TOUGH ON ICE. THE ICE NEEDS TO BE TAKEN CARE OF SO IT'S SMOOTH AND THE PUCK DOESN'T JUMP AROUND ON IT.

OVERTIME

There are no ties in hockey. If the game is tied after three periods, an extra period is played. This is called overtime. The period is different lengths in different leagues. The first team to score in overtime wins the game.

ONE ON ONE

In some leagues, if the score is still tied after overtime, they have a shootout. Each team picks three players who each get one shot on the other team's goalie. Whichever team scores more goals wins!

24

SCORING AN OVERTIME GOAL IS A DREAM FOR MANY HOCKEY PLAYERS.

JOONAS DONSKOI CELEBRATES HIS GAME-WINNING OVERTIME GOAL.

LEARN THE LINGO

Overtime periods where the first goal wins the game are sometimes called "sudden victory" periods, but most people say "sudden death" because it sounds scarier!

DON'T DO THAT!

When a player does something against the rules, they're called for a penalty. The referee then sends them to the penalty box. Most penalties last 2, 4, or 5 minutes. While the player is in the penalty box, their team is shorthanded. They have to play with one less player on the ice.

BOARDING PENALTY SIGNAL ▶

SHORTHANDED TEAMS WITH FOUR PLAYERS ON THE ICE OFTEN MAKE A BOX TO BETTER DEFEND THE NET. WHEN THEY HAVE THREE PLAYERS, THEY OFTEN FORM A TRIANGLE.

THE POWER

Teams put out their best goal scorers when the other team is shorthanded. This time of 5-on-4 hockey is called a "power play."

ANDREW LADD AND BLAKE WHEELER SERVE TIME IN THE PENALTY BOX.

LEARN THE LINGO

If two players are in the penalty box, the power play is called a "two-man advantage."

DIG IN!

Now you know the basics of hockey, but it's just a start! Did you know that when a player scores three goals in a game, it's called a hat trick? And when they score three goals in a row, it's a natural hat trick!

HOME		TIME		GUEST
03		1:23		00
PLAYER	PENALTY	PERIOD 3	PLAYER 21	PENALTY
SHOTS ON GOAL 29	T.O.L. 1	T.O.L. 1		SHOTS ON GOAL 19

LEARN THE LINGO

When a goaltender doesn't allow a goal in a game, it's called a shutout.

HELPING OUT

One important statistic, or stat, in hockey is the assist. That's the pass made by a player before someone scores a goal. Two players can get assists on a goal.

WHEN SOMEONE SCORES A HAT TRICK, HOME TEAM FANS THROW HATS ON THE ICE TO CELEBRATE!

GLOSSARY

celebrate: to honor with special activities

equipment: tools, clothing, and other items needed for a job

fiberglass: a type of plastic using small threads of glass to make it stronger

glide: to move in a smooth and graceful way

logo: a design or symbol that stands for something

material: something used to make something, such as fabric

neutral: not belonging to or favoring either side in a contest

opponent: the person or team you must beat to win a game

professional: one who earns money from an activity many people do for fun. Also, earning money from an activity many people do for fun

referee: an official who makes sure players follow the rules

temper: to make harder using heat and cold

vulcanized: to harden rubber to make it stronger

FOR MORE INFORMATION

BOOKS

Kortemeier, Todd. *Pro Hockey by the Numbers*. North Mankato, MN: Capstone Press, 2016.

Luke, Andrew. *Ice Hockey*. Broomall, PA: Mason Crest, 2017.

Nagelhout, Ryan. *The Science of Hockey*. New York, NY: PowerKids Press, 2016.

WEBSITES

The Basics
coyotes.nhl.com/club/page.htm?id=32696
Learn more about hockey's basic rules and terms on the Arizona Coyotes website.

Hockey: Rules
ducksters.com/sports/hockeyrules.php
Learn more about the rules of hockey here.

Rule Book
nhlofficials.com/rules.asp
Find the official NHL rule book here.

INDEX